By Joseph Olsen

POETRY

24 Hours
Between Us And Imagination

24 Hours

24 Hours

POEMS

Joseph Olsen

FORMATION PRESS
NEW YORK

Formation Press
Hudson Valley, New York
www.FormationPress.com

For Amy

Abstain from you? Never!
I'd perish swiftly from lack of love.

Contents

Introduction

The Internet is an answer machine, it doesn't help us ask better questions, it only feeds the illusion that we already know everything we need to know to be well-informed. Information sits right at our fingertips and some people (at least some I've encountered) accept information on the Internet as the end all. Content on being so well-informed by a swift Google search, they'll wave off anyone with first-hand experience. In my humble opinion, nothing beats first-hand experience. A teaching of Gnosis, a Greek word which refers to knowledge that one acquires through one's own experience, as opposed to knowledge we have heard or been told.

Take dry fasting for instance, (My segue into the introduction of this book) where one abstains from any food or liquids for a period of time. I was at a friend's home and mentioned that I was coming off a 24 hour dry fast as I poured myself a glass of water at his kitchen sink. He immediately fumbled for his *smart* phone in his pocket, blurting out, "That's not healthy!"

"I've dry fasted every Sunday for the last two years now," I said, chuckling. "And feel healthier than I have ever felt before."

My friend became rigid as he searched the Internet on his phone, disregarding my statement.

We then sat in the living room with other friends. A few minutes later he looked up from his phone with a smirk and said, "You're going to get muscle loss. It says so here."

"Again, I've been dry fasting every week now for the last two years." I said. "In fact, I've gained more lean muscle than I've ever had before."

I then asked what he wanted from our conversation. "Do you want me to tell you the benefits I *experience* from dry fasting or do you want to think you're right?"

There was a moment of awkward silence before another friend laughed at something on the (muted) television, ending our conversation.

I amassed information on the miraculous potential fasting had to heal the body, not from the Internet, but from a number of books and conversations with people who had first-hand experience.

The art of fasting is an ancient tradition practiced for thousands of years for curing illness of all kinds, rejuvenation, clarity and decision making, cleansing and strengthening. Have you noticed that when you're sick, your appetite diminishes? (Similarly, when animals are ill, they lie down and often don't eat or drink.) Energy goes towards healing our bodies instead of digesting food.

I was very sick as a child. A preemie with underdeveloped lungs. I suffered constantly from severe asthma attacks and in my twenties, I endured years of panic attacks.

Over the last two years of periodically dry fasting my immune system progressively strengthened. I've experienced how fasting allows the body's enzyme system to focus on detoxifying and breaking down toxins in the body quickly and efficiently without the job of heavy food digestion.

I abandoned fear I let others fill my head with and moved out of my body's way. It is amazing what it's capable of. All ailments I suffered were now nonexistent. With a clean bill of health from my doctor, I continue to abstain from food and water every Sunday.

One Sunday I went beyond my norm and stood awake for 24 hours in addition to abstaining from food and water and contemplated my existence through writing. Every hour I opened my journal and wrote a poem, sometimes two. I've also written Pops (Haiku's called Pops by Jack Kerouac) on some hours.

It's been an experience I will cherish over and over again now that I have this book!

I've abstained from food, water and sleep for 24 hours,
these are the poems I wrote.

"Don't think about what can happen
in a month. Don't think about what
can happen in a year. Just focus
on the 24 hours in front of you
and do what you can to get
closer to where you want to be."

-Eric Thomas

24 Hours

Redeemed by the light of day
Of His sun above
Manifested from His unconditional love
Blooming the roses of emotion
Of angelic notion

Intuited by the opening phases
Of His moon above
Transcendent in the wisdom of His courtly love
The roses of emotion deflowers
Of flesh that was never ours

The soul, poised within a wheel
Of His powers
Turning every 24 hours
Toward a future of grave dissent
Shedding the body
Eternally present

1st Hour 7-8 p.m.

"Scars have the strange power to
remind us that our past is real."

−Cormac McCathy

Into My Heart

I've vacated my thoughts
Into the ether
Leaving my higher self
To pan through them
Like a gold miner
Placing back
Into my heart
The ones gleaming
24 karat love

7:45 p.m.

"Enjoy yourself.
It's later than you think."

-Chinese proverb

So Much Longer
For Amy

I want to hold her
So much longer
Than the shallow
Grip of ego on her personality
To embrace her with spiritual superiority
Emptied of flesh
Filled with her romance

I want to hold her
So much longer
Than I have

2nd Hour 8-9 p.m.

"They always say time changes things,
but you actually have to change them yourself."

-Andy Warhol

Via Cellular Phone

My brother, via cellular phone
With choppy service and the voice
Of a malfunctioning robot, said,
"Mom's been taken."
Then he cut out.

"Kidnapped?"
I inquired nervously into the device.
His voice returned through a tin can, saying,
"No,
"Taken to the emergency room."

Then he cut out again
And waiting for his voice to return
(Which never did)
I couldn't stop thinking
Disownment is unjust
Lamenting twenty years
Of envisioned rekindling
As it flat-lined
With a long, drawn out BEEEEEEEEP
Coming from the cellular phone
Like an electrocardiogram
When there's no heartbeat

"In the chair
I decide to call Haiku
By the name of Pop"

-Jack Kerouac

Pops 1-11

1.

Desk, lamp-lit
Beneath artificial light
I write

2.

The Art Of Simple Food. The Art
Of Loving. The Meaning Of Happiness
Bestsellers

3.

I swallow saliva
In an attempt
To quench my thirst

4.

Thank you, Father; all that
You are, I am; all that you have
Is mine

5.

A young man stands on the edge
Of a cliff on a new adventure
What a fool!

6.

Proverbs 4:1
The Bible
Bookmarked

7.

She said, "I want to learn
How to read palms."
I said, "Take my hand."

8.

I was
Once
Younger then

9.

I think about her
What is valued
The mind's inner camera records

10.

Emptiness
Fills me like a dream
I've woken up from

11.

Safe for who
To trust? Safe for who
To not?

4th Hour 10-11 p.m.

"The best thing one can do
when it is raining
is to let it rain."

-Henry Wadsworth Longfellow

Nimbostratus

Forecasters in
The Hudson valley, New York
Advised residents
To prepare for rain showers
By cleaning gutters
And downspouts
Checking for leaks
And sealing on doors
And replacing HVAC filters.

I surveyed my rented apartment;
The gutters were clogged
Their downspouts detached.
A draft chilled the bedroom
From unsealed doors
And no HVAC existed
To replace filters.

I sat at my writing desk
And like depleted nimbostratus clouds
I prepared
To be full again

10:45 p.m.

"Waste no time arguing
what a good person should be.
Be one."

-Marcus Aurelius

Renewal Of Faith

In a renewal of faith
The poet let go
Free-fell
Through a void
Of rebirth

Caught by God
The poet was placed
Into the bosom of existence

The poet began suckling
Writing another
Poem

5th Hour 11-12 p.m.

"Time is an illusion."

-Albert Einstein

( )

You (The world)
Have trapped me in cages
Of day and night
Ego and mind
Love and hate

For far too long
I've been pacing back and forth
In and out of duality

No more day and night
No more ego and mind
No more love and hate
No more wasting away

You (Me)
Lift the veil
And break free
Running, running
Running in joyous freedom

11:11 p.m.

"Here we are, trapped in the
amber of the moment. There is no why."

-Kurt Vonnegut

Eleven Eleven

Divinely guided
Through His word
God nourishes me

I become full
In a way only a soul
Can become full
Leaving its flesh
Hollow

6th Hour 12-1 a.m.

"Time is a created thing.
To say, 'I don't have time',
is like saying, I don't want to'."

-Lao Tzu

Through Abstinence

Through abstinence
I become no one

No one to witness
The miracle of my body heal itself
Through abstinence
No one to experience
My thoughts sync with the divine mind
Through abstinence
No one to heed
My higher self express himself
Through abstinence
No one to sense
My breath sustain consciousness
Through abstinence
No one to push
The pen across the page in poetic advance

Through abstinence
I become no one

7th Hour 1-2 a.m.

"You may delay, but time will not wait."

-Benjamin Franklin

In The Still Of Mourning

In the still of mourning
The dead of night
He looked strangely
At everything in his sight

Could emptiness be filled with the potential
To muse unrestrained prose of love to an aging heart?

In the still of mourning
The dead of night
Everything in his sight
Looked strangely

1:11 p.m.

```
"Time is a game played
beautifully by children."
```

-Heraclitus, Fragments

Omnipresent Applause

If you would
Listen with intention
To the miracle of recognition
God renders
In omnipresent applause
You'd hear the sound
Of one hand clapping

8th Hour 2-3 a.m.

"Time is what we want most,
but what we use worst."

-William Penn

O Abstinence

O Abstinence, your vacancy
Is a blessing
I feel all the stars in the sky

O Abstinence, your emptiness
Exceeds purported benefits
I know myself in the motion of the planets

O Abstinence, your formlessness
Nourishes awareness
I am conscious *I* exist

O Abstinence, your nothingness
Renders me no name
I am nobody, I confess

O Abstinence, your evanescence
Has awakened me
I discover God in the bosom of night
Painting moonlight

9th Hour   3-4 a.m.

"The future is uncertain but the end
is always near."

–Jim Morrison

No Word

There's been
No word
On the seriousness of mom's
Hospital stay

As if a word could describe
The ineffable severity
Of her disownment of me
(Of the ten of us)

This ninth hour wrenches from my
Mind the sixth month
Evicted from her womb

As if a verb could describe
The ineffable strain of a first breath
Painstakingly drawn by mom's favorite son
Desperate to announce his souls embodiment

My ego projects regret

As if the phrase could describe
The ineffable seriousness of mom's
Hospital stay
There's been
No word

10th Hour 4-5 a.m.

"Time takes it all,
whether you want it to or not."

-Stephen King

12.

Five hundred and
Forty minutes expired
Mindfully

13.

Playing time
Against my
Troubles

14.

A member of
The death club
We will all wear the jacket

15.

Buddha is laughing
Belly protruding
The divine comedy

16.

The woodpecker will be
Here at dawn
Who's knocking now?

17.

Always a writer
A poet
Forever

18.

Intuition -
Nutrition
For abstinence

19.

Pursuing consciousness
Sleeping awake
Dreaming

20.

Prematurely born
Ahead of my time
Maturely dying

21.

How to live poetically;
Wake. Love. Sleep. Dream
Repeat

22.

Between Us And Imagination
Souls suit up
For this physical dimension

11th Hour 5-6 a.m.

"The strongest of all warriors are
these two - Time and Patience."

-Leo Tolstoy

Dozed

I dozed off
For five minutes I dreamed
I was sleeping
Dreaming I was asleep

In no way would I have
Figured out
I was actually awake
Day dreaming I was asleep
Dreaming I was sleeping
If I hadn't dozed off

12th Hour 6-7 a.m.

"Muddy water is best cleared
by leaving it alone."

-Alan Watts

The Art Of Letting Go

The moon's
A waning gibbous
Dissipating fog
Paints dawn
With morning light
The art
Of letting go

13th Hour 7-8 a.m.

"Time is what keeps everything
from happening all at once."

-Ray Cummings

Superstitious

Seconds to minutes
Competing to outlast
A superstitious hour
Came ticking along

The nature of poetry
Is not in the grammar, but in the gut.

A fasting theme
A child's scene
Seeing the face of my father
Who is in heaven

The nature of time
Is not in reality, but in the illusion

Of minutes to seconds
Competing to outlast
A superstitious hour
Came ticking along

14th Hour 8-9 a.m.

"Clocks slay time...time is dead as long
as it is being clicked off by little wheels;
only when the clock stops does time
come to life."

—William Faulkner

The Sun Rises

With prestige and esoteric beauty
The sun rises
Its golden rays methodically
Filling darkness with its light

I face east
Like a young flower
Greeting the solar disc
Then I switch off my desk lamp
No longer in need
Of artificial luminance
Or the ego's
Mis-education
Of consciousness

"And indeed there will be time
to wonder, "Do I dare?""

−T.S. Eliot

The Bronx, Resigned

You can take the cat out of the jungle
But you can't take the jungle out of the cat

The Bronx
Resigned

Nowadays the Hudson valley encompasses me
Worshiping rurally
Petitioning God in fields
With prayers from the old blocks
Invoking my inner child playing in roads
Games from the old streets

The Bronx
A frame of mind

Hanging in the Hudson valley
Contemplating no food, no water, no sleep
In concrete consciousness
The Boogie Down adorned with my past
In present moment awareness
Meaningfully designed

The Bronx
Resigned

"Until you value yourself, you won't value
your time. Until you value your time,
you will not do anything with it."

-M. Scott Peck

I've Denied Myself

I've denied myself
Fled from flesh
Toward faith
And spirituality

Taking up my cross
And following Him

"Inelegantly, and without my consent
time passed."

-Miranda July

23.

Thankful at birth
The dead say,
"Hello."

24.

Remembering the Frost of my twenties
Leaving behind the Whitman of my thirties
Welcoming the Ferlinghetti of my forties

25.

Inspired light
Here and now
The present moment

26.

Everything spirit touches
Surrenders
This human experience

27.

Kaleidoscope of spirituality
Divine presence
Never changes

28.

The cafe Baristas
Haven't a clue
Espresso's aroma harasses me

29.

Famished
Mourning
A marvelous feast

30.

The elderly
Are starving
Young

31.

Digital hearts
XOXO 0010 OXOX 1011
Analog desires

32.

Moonlight reads to the night
What the stars
Have written

33.

Thankful at death
The living say,
"Goodbye."

18th Hour 12-1 p.m.

"I have realized that the past and future
are real illusions, that they exist in the
present, which is what there is
and all there is."

-Alan Watts

Nobody Knows

They see you writing
They see your words
They see you contemplating
The distance between dreams and their *real* world
They see you in artificial light
They see you as they want to see themselves
They see you as their calloused hearts
They see you as their forgotten counterparts
They see you as their prayers for unconditional love
You see?
The seers; they don't know
Nobody knows
Not even you

19th Hour 1-2 p.m.

"With endless time, nothing is special.
With no loss or sacrifice,
we can't appreciate what we have."

–Mitch Albom

Ordinary Things

Ordinary people are doing
Ordinary things
Angels without typical wings
Performing miracles like ancient kings
Writing of earthly paradise springs
This is why the caged bird sings;
Ordinary people are doing
Ordinary things

"Time's the thief of memory."

-Stephen King

The End Of A Song

Elvis is on the radio
Abusing me
Like he and my father did
When I was a child.
Dad's flaming breath of scotch
And his large fists
In tune with Elvis' beat of Jailhouse Rock.
Oh, how they struck me
Then left me to die.

But I'm still here
While Elvis has left the building
And dad
Somewhere in the world
Heavy headed and numb
Fading out
Like the end of a song.

21st Hour 3-4 p.m.

"Three o'clock is always too late or too
early for anything you want to do."

-Jean-Paul Sartre

Hunger Pangs

They say the gnawing
Painful feelings in my gut
Are parasites screaming out
For sustenance.

I have not come this far
To satiate the old beggars
No matter the grief
Or hunger pangs.

22nd Hour 4-5 p.m.

"Time is precious, but truth is more
precious than time."

-Benjamin Disraeli

On Overhead Wires

Look up
And you will notice
Birds on overhead wires
In a frenzy of opinion
Regurgitating
Nourishing their young
Swooping for more crumbs
Then flying off
Landing
On overhead wires.

And on rare occasions
One will be shocked
You're looking up

23rd Hour 5-6 p.m.

"It is looking at things for a long time
that ripens you and gives you a deeper meaning."

-Vincent van Gogh

34.

It's never
Too late
For words

35.

The stars sympathize
For the moon
Enduring a waning gibbous phase

36.

Contemplate thyself
Regularly
Color auras vividly

37.

Look with the mind's eye
The center of your chest
Heart Chakra

38.

Conditioned by actions
During this life's
Karma

39.

Effective magic
Writing
Poetry

40.

Should I take
My last breath
And keep it for myself?

41.

If Grandpa was a pull string doll
He'd say,
"Why lie?"

42.

Yahweh buried enlightenment
Under an unmarked
Ancient sacred fig tree

43.

Back to
The light of existence
From the darkness of meditation

44.

This haiku
Goes
Pop

24th Hour 6-7 p.m.

"Time will explain."

-Jane Austen

Darkness Into light

Hear with me
Moonshine sounds
The saints
Come marching in
Mercilessly scorching sin
Forming the stars within
Conscious dreams
Skipping across the firmament
Further into the night
Breathing darkness
Into light.

"How did it get so late so soon?
It's night before it's afternoon.
December is here before it's June.
My goodness how the time has flewn.
How did it get so late so soon?"

-Dr. Seuss

Breaking (Fast) Bad

I've broken
24 hours
Of abstinence
With the inky dark color
And Argentinian taste
Of a glass of red
A large house salad with balsamic vinaigrette
A bowl of Penne Alla Vodka
15oz of pistachios, shelled one by one
A grilled Swiss Cheese on Rye
And 2 liters of spring water.

What I did afterward was
Thank God for rest
And the blessing of organs
To replenish
And digest.

7:35 p.m.

"You need to make time for your family
no matter what happens in your life."

-Matthew Quick

What Happened To Mom

Out of the clearest blue wintry day
Mom tumbled on black ice
Like a cartoon character
Head over heals
Slipping on a banana peel
Splitting open her head.

Under the blaring surgical lights of the
Hospital operating room
Doctors in white
Stapled her pink flesh back together
Temporarily mending her wounded prefrontal cortex
Prompting her ten children she disowned
Twenty years ago
To flash in her mind.
With crocodile tears
She professed pseudo love for us to a nurse
Without invitation to draw us near
To mend the beat of our creator's
Unclaimed heart.

10 p.m.

"When you are measuring life,
you are not living it."

-Mitch Albom

45.

Who in your body
Is the pain
You suffer?

46.

On my own
Alone
In the window's reflection

47.

Satori may be
Described as
Ineffable

48.

Satan is privy
To the location of the keys
To heaven's gates

49.

Each of us are
Characters in the stories
Of the Holy Scriptures

50.

Heaven is a birdcage
The angels
Sing

51.

On silent hinges
Spirit enters through
The other, other door

52.

I witness myself
Observe writing
Dissolving the ego

53.

His name
Everyone knows. The poet
No one writes to

54.

Somebody
Somewhere
Time of death

55.

Time after
Time and
Again

"Men talk of killing time, while time quietly kills them."

-Dion Boucicault

Acknowledgments

As always
I have valued the insights and comments
I've received while working on these poems.

A special thank you to Amy;
To my sons, Nicholas and Alexander;
To my brother, Danny;
To Marilyn Kline,
Robert Milby,
Donna Cornell,
and Norman Trager.

Printed in the USA
CPSIA information can be obtained
at www.ICGtesting.com
JSHW082229111223
53498JS00004B/181